Silver Flatware Dictionary

Silver Flatware Dictionary

Richard F. Osterberg
and
Betty Smith

*Photographs by Douglas Dill
and Jim Heitzeberg*

San Diego • New York
A. S. Barnes & Company, Inc.
In London:
The Tantivy Press

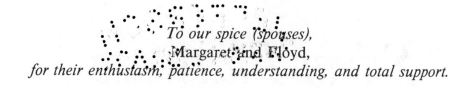

*To our spice (spouses),
Margaret and Floyd,
for their enthusiasm, patience, understanding, and total support.*

First Edition
Manufactured in the United States of America

For information write to:
A.S. Barnes & Company, Inc.
P.O. Box 3051
La Jolla, California 92038

The Tantivy Press
Magdalen House
136-148 Tooley Street
London, SE1 2TT, England

Library of Congress Cataloging in Publication Data

Osterberg, Richard F.   1938-
Silver flatware dictionary.

Includes index.
1. Silverware — Dictionaries.   I.   Smith, Betty,
1927-   joint author.   II.   Title.
NK7104.077   739.2'383   78-75323
ISBN 0-498-02327-3

2 3 4 5 6 7 8 9 84 83 82

Contents

Acknowledgments

We wish to express our thanks to the following individuals for helping us with the Index of Manufacturers:

Robert T. Bown, Secretary, International Silver Company, Meriden, Connecticut.

Robert Crone, Gorham Company, Providence, Rhode Island.

John J. Hamilton, Director of Product Development, Wallace Silversmiths, Wallingford, Connecticut.

L. S. Hoagland, Tiffany and Company, New York, New York.

Robert M. Johnston, The Stieff Company, Baltimore, Maryland.

A. La Chapelle and Alan E. Voll, Reed and Barton Corporation, Taunton, Massachusetts.

Denham C. Lunt, Jr., Lunt Silversmiths, Greenfield, Massachusetts.

S. K. Milspaugh, Kirk Company, Baltimore, Maryland.

Daniel Prouty, Operations Manager, Shreve and Company, San Francisco, California.

Arthur L. Roy, Towle Silversmiths, Newburyport, Massachusetts.

Phebe McAlpine Shepard, President, Manchester Silver Company, Providence, Rhode Island.

Special thanks to Jane Breckenridge Palmatier for typing, editing, and encouragement.

Preface

Having first met—frequently—in various antique shops and at antique shows, attempting to best one another for the most desirable "odd" pieces of silver, the authors soon decided that friendly collaboration was a more satisfactory avenue of pursuit than self-seeking competition. This book is a result of that long and productive friendly collaboration between the two of them. The authors can now claim an aggregate of forty years of silver collecting.

Early discussions soon led us to the discovery of mutual interests in food, table settings, and entertaining. Cooking and serving good food, and attractively using our various collections of silver, china, glassware, and accessories, became our primary interest. The Osterbergs specialized in gourmet dinners and formal table settings, serving multiple courses. The Smiths preferred the extremely casual, mixing patterns and textures and limiting the number of tableware pieces used, but always emphasizing "the collections." We have each learned from the other.

In today's casual and less complicated way of life, most formal dinners have become less so, and many innovations and variations are not only permitted, but indeed, are encouraged. We believe, whatever your inclinations may be, that either formal or casual dining can be elegant—perhaps utilizing those few pieces of fine silver and china that Aunt Martha left you in combination with some interesting "everyday" items, cleverly and thoughtfully arranged. It is fun—and useful—to know that that great big spoon with all the piercing is a "Pea Spoon" and that it can be perfectly at home today serving coleslaw or potato salad instead of residing permanently in the cedar chest. A favorite maxim of ours is: "Once you know the rules, you may break them!" Our only hard-and-fast edict, however, is: "If it serves the purpose, it is correct."

We neither pretend nor profess to be experts. In some cases we are, frankly, guessing at original usage. (And how we would welcome information from those of you who formerly dined in Edwardian splendor at a table brilliant with Aspic Slicers, Horseradish Spoons, Fish Serving Sets, Strawberry Forks, and Ice Scoops, and who might be able to help us identify questionable pieces.) We have learned by studying and reading everything we could get our hands on. Almost invariably, when we finally reached a conclusion or agreed on something, we would find a contradiction—just as we shall undoubtedly be contradicted. Our intent, however, is not only to inform: it is to inspire.

The Authors

P. O. Box 5118
Fresno, California, 93755
March 31, 1979

Silver Flatware Dictionary

PART I

Serving Pieces

Introduction to Part I

Nothing reflects elegance, good taste, and lasting beauty more than sterling. There is no substitute. It should not be hidden away to be used only on "special occasions," but should be used daily—perhaps to make a "special occasion" of each day. With daily use, sterling silver requires only a minimum of care and becomes more beautiful. What is more fun than a casual, yet elegant, buffet, brunch, picnic, or barbecue utilizing nice things, rather than paper and plastic so often associated with these kinds of parties?

Fewer pieces of sterling flatware are being made today than made in the past, but there are still more than enough to confuse all but the expert, thus enabling the silver companies to narrow down the number of specialized pieces they produce. This policy, however, merely spurs the collector to greater endeavors in acquiring those great old pieces no longer being made. Only too frequently, however, when a magnificent piece is found, one is really stumped as to exactly what to do with it, since one doesn't really know what it was designed for originally.

Formerly, each manufacturer had a favorite shape—and not infrequently, size and classification—for specialized pieces, and we have found many variations. For example, a "Fried Oyster Server" made by one company may be called a "Tomato Server" by another, an "Entrée Server" by another, or a "Cheese Server" by still another—yet all may be identical or similar in shape and size. On the other hand, one company's "Pastry Server" may be entirely dissimilar to another company's "Pastry Server." We have attempted to show a variety of pieces by a variety of companies within individual categories to illustrate this point.

We have also listed, following the pattern name, a numeral which indicates the size of the particular piece. The measurements have been taken in a consistent manner, that is, by placing the piece face down on a ruler; they are accurate to within the nearest $1/8$ inch.

We hope that this picture dictionary will serve its intended purpose, and that you will find an immediate use for that curious-looking fork that you received as a wedding gift.

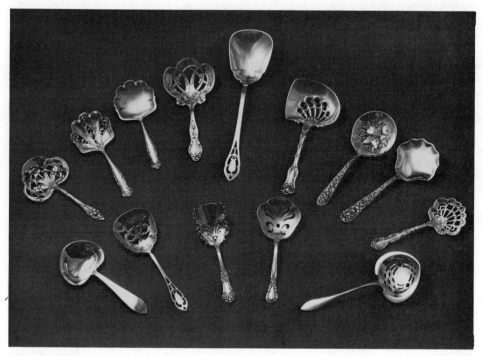

Left to right:
Top row: Floral, 4⅝″ (Gorham); Canterbury [Bon Bon], 4½″ (Towle); Canterbury [nut], 4½″ (Towle); Violet, 4⅝″ (Wallace); Pierced Handle [Nut], 6¼″ (Manchester); Imperial Queen, 5½″ (Whiting); Repousse, 5½″ (Kirk); Rose, 5½″ (Stieff); Strasbourg, 4⅜″ (Gorham).
Bottom row: Faneuil, 4⅝″ (Tiffany); Pierced Handle, 6½″ (Manchester); Olympia, 4½″ (Watson); Chantilly, 4⅝″ (Gorham); Lafayette, 6¼″ (Towle).

Almond, Nut, and Bonbon Spoons

Not to be overlooked at holiday times for added sparkle at the festive board are *Almond* or *Nut Scoops/Spoons,* or *Bonbon Spoons.* The variety of styles and sizes allows for a diversity of uses. Dried fruit is easily served with this handy implement. Larger sizes, sometimes called confection spoons, can be used for popcorn, nut and cereal mixes, fruits, candy, mints, croutons, and oyster crackers. Those which are flatter are useful for serving broiled or sliced tomatoes, croquettes, stuffed mushrooms, stuffed and/or marinated vegetables, some pastries, or for providing a sprinkle of Parmesan cheese or powdered sugar.

4

Asparagus Servers or Asparagus Forks

A unique large fork designed with a specific purpose, the *Asparagus Fork* can be used—in addition to serving hot or cold asparagus—for meats, meat patties, scallopini, chops, sautéed eggplant, moussaka, squash, molded salads, waffles, hot cakes, Danish pastry, fish, stuffed cabbage rolls, lasagna, and other casseroles. This piece is indispensable on the buffet table.

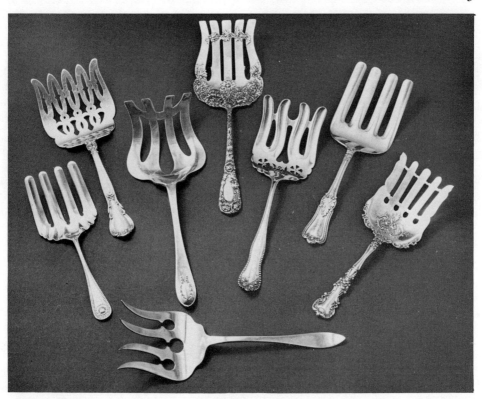

Left to right:
Top row: Bead, 7¼″ (Whiting); Chantilly, 8½″ (Gorham); Napoleonic, 9¾″ (Shreve); Chrysanthemum, 9¾″ (Durgin); Lancaster, 9⅜″ (Gorham); Kensington, 9⅛″ (Gorham); Avalon, 8¼″ (Simpson, Hall and Miller/International).
Bottom row: Buckingham [Toast Fork (?), Fish Fork (?), Salad Serving Fork (?)], 9¼″ (Shreve).

Aspic Slicer

Apparently, *Aspic Slicers* were for the hostess who had everything, as they were made in exclusive patterns only. The Slicer is a large, sickle-shaped piece that worked well for slicing through a large ring mold of aspic or "calves' foot jelly." Baked Alaska, large molded bombes, or frozen or jellied mousses are suggested for present-day use of the Slicer. Otherwise, it is a lovely piece to own and look at.

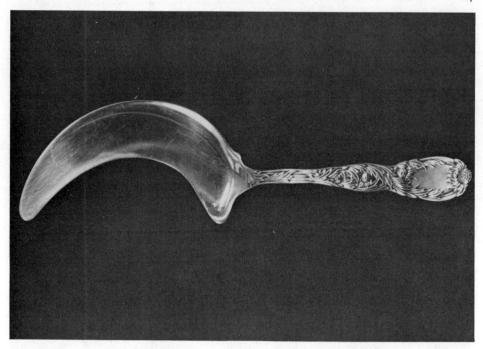

Chrysanthemum, 11″ (Tiffany).

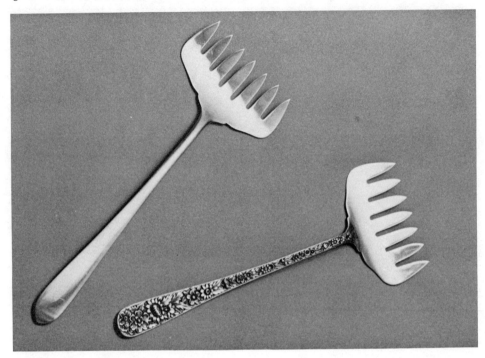

Top: Wadefield, 7¾″ (Kirk).
Bottom: Repousse, 7¾″ (Kirk).

Bacon Forks

Bacon Forks were formerly—and are still—made in only a few patterns. They are perfect for serving dolma and sarma (stuffed grape leaves), sausages, whole baby carrots, braised celery, asparagus, French fried potatoes, whole green beans, baked or sautéed bananas, eclairs, and small party crêpes.

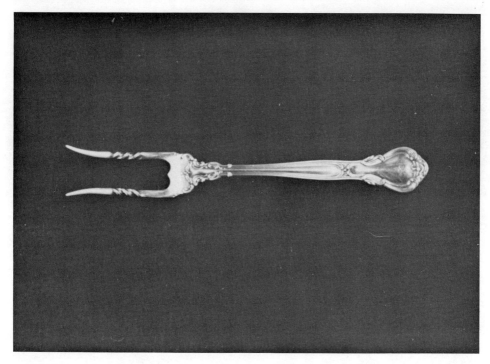

Chantilly, 7⅛" (Gorham).

Baked Potato or Sandwich Fork

Most *Baked Potato* or *Sandwich Forks* seen by us to date were made by Gorham in turn-of-the-century patterns only, although old catalogues of other companies list them. Perfectly designed for their original purposes, they can also be used for serving sliced or stuffed meats, stuffed tomatoes, rolls, spiced peaches, pastries, and even petits fours.

Beef Forks

Beef Forks come in two sizes: large and small. They can be used to serve sliced cheeses and all cold cuts, canapés, meat patties, chops, broiled tomatoes, baked or boiled potatoes, grilled onions, terrines, stuffed mushrooms, meringues, strudel, petits fours, some Danish pastries, cream puffs, and gooey sticky desserts such as baklava.

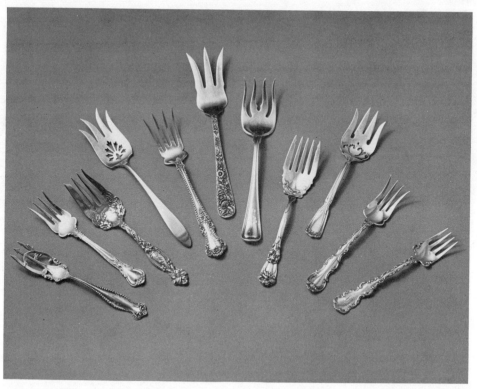

Left to right:
Canterbury, 6¼″ (Towle); Chantilly, 5⅞″ (Gorham); Frontenac, 6½″ (Simpson, Hall and Miller/International); Unidentified pattern, 7⅞″ (unidentified maker); Cambridge, 6⅞″ (Gorham); Repousse, 7⅞″ (Kirk); Old French, 7⅛″ (Gorham); Iris, 6½″ (Durgin); Chambord, 5¾″ (Reed and Barton); Strasbourg, 5¼″ (Gorham); Louis XV, 5¾″ (Whiting).

12
Berry Spoons

With elegant large bowls—occasionally pierced—these spoons can be used for berries, compotes, and melon balls. They are also well designed for serving stews, beef bourguigonne, baked bean dishes, casseroles, potato and macaroni salads, curry dishes, some pilaf and pasta dishes, baked apples and various puddings, custards, and ice cream. No buffet table should be complete without at least one *Berry Spoon.*

Left to right:
Top row: Strasbourg, 7⅝″ (Gorham); Orange Blossom, 9⅜″ (Alvin); Chrysanthemum [large], 9½″ (Durgin); Repousse [large], 9¼″ (Kirk).
Bottom row: King George, 7½″ (Gorham); Henry II, 9″ (Gorham); New Art, 9″ (Durgin); Chrysanthemum [medium], 9⅛″ (Durgin); Repousse [medium], 7⅝″ (Kirk).

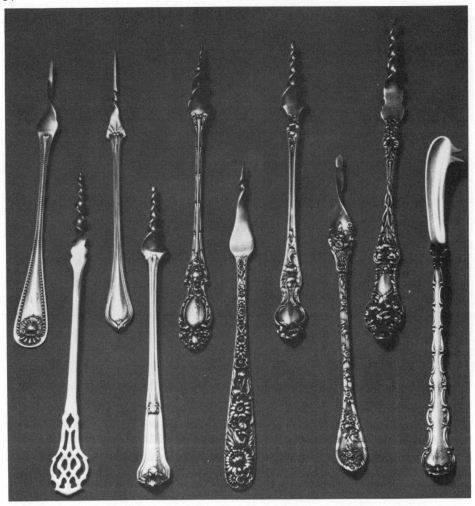

Left to right:
Top row: Bead, 5⅝″ (Whiting); Paul Revere, 5⅝″ (Towle); Lucerne, 6″ (Wallace); Violet, 6″ (Wallace); Orange Blossom, 6½″ (Alvin).
Bottom row: Chippendale, 6½″ (Lunt); Corinthian, 6″ (Wallace); Repousse, 6⅛″ (Kirk); Dauphin, 6⅛″ (Durgin): Strasbourg; 6¼″ [note different style] (Gorham).

Butter Picks

Remember when Grandma made individual butter balls or curls and served them on ice with her *Butter Pick?* Wonderful still for serving ice-cold butter balls or butter pats, Butter Picks could also be used for serving pickles, pickled beets, olives, herring, mushrooms, cheese balls, hors d'oeuvres, tiny meatballs, shrimp, sausages, and dried stuffed fruit. A collector lucky enough to have several may use them for serving fondues, especially dessert fondues.

15

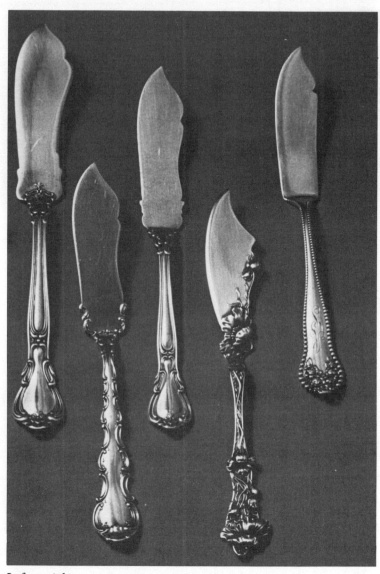

Left to right:
Chantilly, 7⅛″ (Gorham); Strasbourg, 6⅞″ (Gorham); Chantilly [small], 6⅞″ (Gorham); Poppy, 6⅞″ (Paye and Baker); Lancaster, 6″ (Gorham).

Butter Serving Knives

Aside from their primary use with butter, additional uses for *Butter Serving Knives* could be with cheese, cheese spreads, pâtés, terrines, some jellies, and on smorgasbord tables or canapé trays. Larger ones could be teamed with a fork of compatible size, to serve fish or meatloaf.

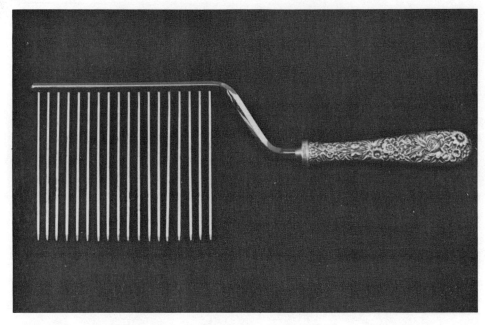

Repousse, 10¾″ (Kirk).

CAKE SERVERS (see also Pastry and Pie Servers; Ice Cream Servers)

Cake Breakers

The use of *Cake Breakers* is usually limited to breaking apart lightly textured cakes such as angel food, sponge, or chiffon cakes without crushing, and they are excellent for this purpose.

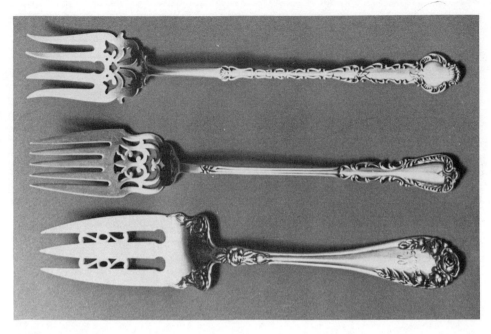

Left to right:
  Rose, 8⅛″ (Wallace); Majestic, 8⅜″ (Reed and Barton); Unidentified pattern, 8⅝″ (Curtis, Glenny, or Waldo[?]).

Cake Forks

Specifically designed for the dessert table for serving cakes and pastries, *Cake Forks* can also be used for serving petits fours, eclairs, patty shells, and individual portions of gelatin salads or molded desserts. Buffet table uses could include serving meats, cheeses, and some international dishes such as manicotti, baklava, and strudel.

Top to bottom:
La Marquise [Cake Knife], 9¼″ (Reed and Barton); Louis XV, 9⅛″ (Whiting); Chantilly, 9½″ (Gorham); Rococo, 9¼″ (Dominick and Haff).

Cake Saws and Cake Knives

Saw teeth on one edge of an all-silver knife identifies a *Cake Saw;* without saw teeth it is usually called a *Cake Knife.* After cutting through the cake, the Saw or Knife may be turned for lifting out the cut piece. It is beautiful on the bride's table, and it works well for cutting and serving other festive cakes, as well as for molded salads.

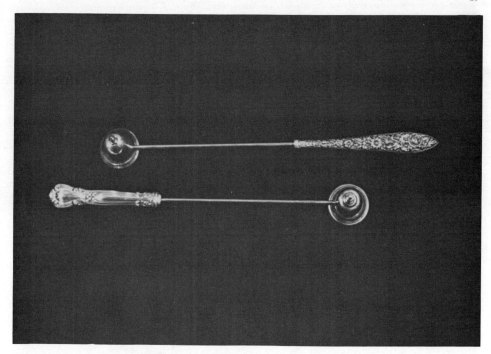

Top: Repousse, 10¾" (Kirk).
Bottom: Chantilly, 8½" (Gorham).

Candlesnuffers

Candlesnuffers are old pieces, made popular by Colonial silversmiths, which were uniquely designed for doing one thing: snuffing out a burning candle quickly so that the liquid wax would not be blown over the linen. They are still available today in many current patterns, and make lovely wedding or anniversary gifts, since they are as decorative as they are useful.

20

Carving Sets

The well-appointed Victorian or Edwardian table had a wide assortment of carving utensils. Items ranged from the *Roast Set* [large], *Steak Set* [medium], to *Game* or *Duck Carving Set* [small]. Also available were *Bone Holders* (not illustrated), *Carver's Assistants* (not illustrated), and *Poultry Shears*.

Designed for cutting hot or cold meats, the knives can be used for cutting the wedding cake. Forks can be used for serving, as well as for assisting the carver, and can be used on the buffet table for items such as baked potatoes. The smaller forks can be used for cold cuts and sliced cheeses.

Poultry Shears are an indispensable tool in the kitchen for cutting up either raw or cooked poultry, and an elegant tool at the table for whole roasted or barbecued chicken, game hens, or turkey.

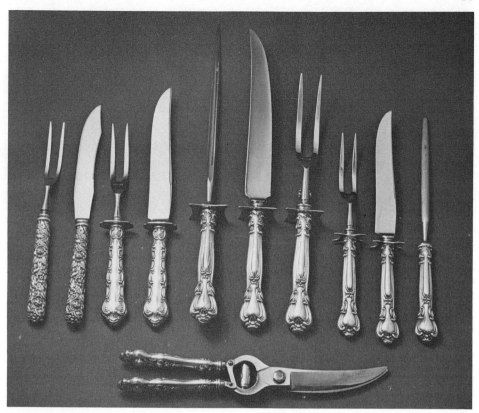

Left to right:
Top row: Two-piece Steak Set: Repousse, Fork, 9″; Knife, 9¾″ (Kirk); Two-piece Steak Set: Strasbourg, Fork, 8⅝″; Knife, 10⅜″ (Gorham); Three-piece Roast Set: Chantilly, Steel, 14¼″; Knife, 13¼″; Fork, 11¼″ (Gorham); Three-piece Steak Set: Chantilly, Fork, 8¾″; Knife, 10″; Steel, 10⅛″ (Gorham).
Bottom row: Poultry Shears: Violet, 10″ (Wallace).

22

Cheese Scoops

Really limited items, *Cheese Scoops* were made in various sizes: larger ones for large crocks of soft cheese and smaller ones for smaller containers. They can be adapted for cottage cheese, Parmesan cheese, pâtés, cranberries, pickles, and relish dishes—and how about a small one for feeding the baby?

Left to right:
Trajan, 6⅛″ (Dominick and Haff); Victoria, 7″ (F. M. Whiting); Repousse, 8⅝″ (Kirk);
Chantilly, 8¼″ (Gorham); Chantilly, 6″ (Gorham); Wedding Rose, 6″ (Watson).

Cheese Servers

The illustration shows several pieces representative of the wide range of shapes and styles of *Cheese Servers.* All the various shapes are usable on the cheese board and on the buffet for spreads, pâtés, terrines, and hors d'oeuvres. Toothed styles can be used for picking up cheese balls or assorted hors d'oeuvres. Small pastries can be served with the wider types.

Left to right:
Strasbourg, 6¾" (Gorham); Princess, 7⅝" (Manchester); Chantilly, 8" (Gorham);
Alice, 6" (Fessenden); Spring Glory, 6" (International).

Chocolate Sets: Muddlers and Spoons

Long handles and small round bowls usually identify *Chocolate Muddlers.* Individual *Chocolate Spoons* are miniatures of the Muddler, usually a bit larger than demitasse spoons. They are shown here as a set because they were almost always used that way: the Muddler for stirring chocolate in lovely old chocolate pots and the small ones accompanying those distinctive tall chocolate cups.

The Muddler makes an ideal bar spoon, or pitcher or lemonade spoon. It is ideally suited to serving relishes from a pickle caster, and canned or preserved apricots, plums, or cherries.

Individual spoons could be used for puddings, ice cream, or eggs; for serving jams and jellies, preserves, mustard, or ketchup; and for hotdog or hamburger fixings in small bowls, as well as with some curry condiments.

Frontenac: Muddler, 8½″; Spoons, 3¾″ (Simpson, Hall and Miller/International).

No. 1, left to right:
Four variations in Strasbourg (Gorham): 6¼", 7⅛", 8⅜", 8⅝". Four variations in Chantilly (Gorham): 8¾", 8", 7⅛", 6½".

Cold Meat and Buffet Forks

Sizes vary from very large to very small and all sizes in between. Older patterns usually are more ornate and sometimes pierced. A *Cold Meat* or *Buffet Fork* is a "must" for serving meats and cold cuts at either dining or buffet tables. It is also suitable for sliced tomatoes, cheeses, meat patties, scallopini,

No. 2, left to right:
Francis I [small], 8″ (Reed and Barton); Burgundy [large], 9¼″ (Reed and Barton); Majestic, 8⅞″ (Reed and Barton); Eloquence, 8⅝″ (Lunt); Unidentified pattern, 7⅝″ (Manchester); Repousse, 8⅝″ (Kirk); Rose, 7⅝″ (Stieff).

rolled stuffed-meat dishes, sautéed whole vegetables, or fruits such as apple slices or peaches to accompany and/or garnish. These forks can be teamed with preserve spoons, tablespoons, or berry spoons for salads, coleslaw, sauerkraut, and Oriental dishes.

Left to right:
Chantilly, 9″ (Gorham); Chrysanthemum, 8¼″ (Durgin); Kings, 9″ (Tiffany); Chantilly, 8⅝″ (Gorham); Strasbourg, 9½″ (Gorham).

Cracker and Ice Spoons and/or Scoops

The most impressive of old unusual serving pieces, *Cracker Scoops* and *Ice Spoons* were usually ornate and sometimes pierced. The serving of Saratoga chips and oyster crackers were two of their original purposes, and Ice Spoons

Napoleonic, (Shreve); Pea Spoon, 8½".

sometimes doubled as Pea Spoons. Although a bit large for serving today's portions, they can be used for salads, casseroles, and fruit compotes, and on a buffet table whenever a large spoon is needed.

Crumb Knives or Crumbers

Maids and butlers serving course after course are a part of the "good old days." *Crumb Knives* were usually accompanied by a brush, or other companion piece, to whisk crumbs from the tablecloth between courses. One long straight edge usually identifies them and makes them perfect for lifting enchiladas, filled and rolled crêpes, or manicotti out of a casserole.

Left to right (all items pictured are all-silver):
Chrysanthemum, 12¾″ (Durgin); Poppy [engraved], 12¾″ (Gorham); Indian, 12¾″ (Whiting); Newcastle, 11¾″ (Gorham); Chantilly, 11⅞″ (Gorham); Strasbourg, 11½″ (Gorham).

No. 1, left to right:
Louis XV: Fork, 8⅞″; Slice, 11⅞″ (Whiting). Chantilly: Fork, 8½″; Slice, 11¾″ (Gorham). Strasbourg: Fork, 8½″; Slice, 11¾″ (Gorham).

Fish Serving Sets

Large *Fish Slices* and their accompanying *Forks* are most impressive on a buffet table beside a whole baked, broiled, or poached fish, but either piece works equally well for casseroles, lasagna, enchiladas, crêpes, and many meat

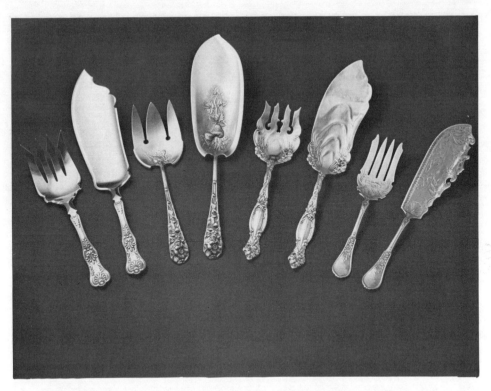

No. 2, left to right:
Kings III: Fork, 8⅝"; Slice, 12" (Gorham). Eglantine: Fork, 9⅛"; Slice, 12½" (Gorham). Frontenac: Fork, 8⅞"; Slice, 12⅜" (Simpson, Hall, and Miller/International). Unidentified pattern: Fork, 8¼"; Slice, 10½" (A. Skinner).

dishes. The Slice can be used also as an auxiliary server for large molded salads or as an extra cake server. Forks can be paired with a large berry spoon or vegetable spoon and used as a salad set or for service on the buffet table whenever a large fork is needed.

No. 1, left to right:
Top row: Dauphin [catalogue listing as "Entrée Server"], 8⅛″ (Durgin); Blossom, 8″ (Dominick and Haff); [handmade hallmarked only Hirschman and Co.] 8″; Chantilly [note raised and decorative edge], 7½″ (Gorham). *Bottom Row:* Chantilly, 7½″ (Gorham), Raleigh, 7⅝″ (Alvin); Strasbourg, 7⅞″ (Gorham); Rose, 7½″ (Stieff); Lafayette, 9″ (Towle).

Flat Servers: Cucumber and Tomato Servers

Each company had its own version of *Cucumber* and *Tomato Servers*— almost always flat and round, the Tomato Server being the larger of the two. Some are toothed or notched and a few are oval or square; some are pierced and some are not—so uses can vary immensely. Still indispensable for tomatoes

No. 2, left to right:
Top row: Repousse, 7″ [Hot Cake Server(?)] (Kirk); Repousse, 7⅝″ (Kirk); Rosalind, 6⅜″ (International).
Bottom Row: Wild Rose, 6″ (Watson); Strasbourg, 6″ (Gorham); Norfolk, 5⅞″ (Gorham); Chantilly, 6⅛″ (Gorham).

and cucumbers, they are also useful for meat patties, fish patties, hot cakes and waffles, croquettes, stuffed vegetables, most entrées and casseroles, chops, fried eggs, folded crêpes, and pastries. Many hostesses consider the flat server as necessary a tool as a tablespoon.

No. 1, left to right:
Ice Cream Ladles (or vegetable spoons): Chantilly, 9½″ (Gorham); Grapevine, 9⅝″ (Tiffany); Grapevine, 11¾″ (Tiffany); Berry pattern, [Berry Spoon], 9¾″ (Tiffany).

Ice Cream Servers: Ice Cream Ladles, Ice Cream Knives

Ice Cream Ladles are unique ladle-shaped pieces that are flat on one side and raised on the other. Of various shapes and sizes, depending on the manufacturer and the pattern, they are nice for molded salads and desserts, frozen desserts, bombes, and baked Alaska. They also can be used for some casseroles and

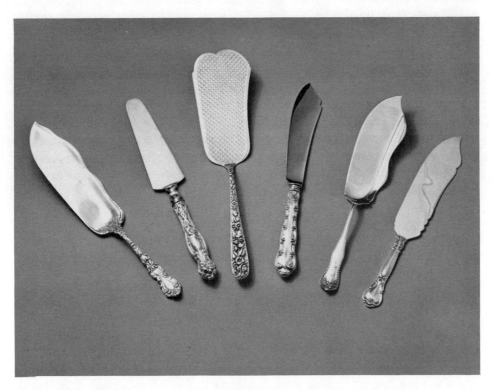

No. 2, left to right:
Ice Cream Knives: Imperial Chrysanthemum [all-silver], 12″ (Gorham); Frontenac [plated blade], 10⅞″ (Simpson, Hall and Miller/International); Repousse [all-silver], 12″ (Kirk); Strasbourg [stainless steel blade], 10⅞″ (Gorham); Lancaster [all-silver], 8⅜″ (Gorham); Chantilly [all-silver and perfectly flat], 10⅛″ (Gorham).

macaroni dishes, such as rigatoni. Some old brochures list them as vegetable spoons; European manufacturers list them as mousse servers.

Ice Cream Knives, originally made for slicing brick and block ice cream, can also be used for slicing bombes, baked Alaska, molded desserts and salads, and as auxiliary cake and pastry servers.

Jam, Jelly, and Honey Spoons

Typically, *Jelly Spoons* or *Servers* have stylized bowl shapes, with the left, or cutting, edge flattened. Many were made in two sizes: the smaller originally for serving molded jelly; the larger, for jellied aspics and "calves' foot jelly." It is an ideal piece for use with molded pâtés, sour cream, jellied cranberry sauce, and ring molds.

Jam Spoons have either round or oval bowls, and *Honey Spoons* have elongated bowls, sometimes with a point to catch the drip. Each substitutes readily for the other. Relishes, chutneys, creamed horseradish, and Bordelaise or other gourmet sauces are some ideas for usage.

Left to right:
Strasbourg, 6⅛″ (Gorham); American Beauty, 6⅜″ (Manchester); Old Maryland Plain, 6¾″ (Kirk); Chantilly [small], 6″ (Gorham); Chantilly [large], 6¾″ (Gorham); Lily of the Valley, 6⅛″ (Gorham); Strasbourg [Jam Spoon], 4⅞″ (Gorham); Lily [Honey Spoon], 6⅛″ (Whiting).

Jelly Knives

Jellied ring molds and aspics were originally served with *Jelly Knives.* Ideal for that purpose, they can be used as well with many pastries and steamed puddings and are perfect for cheese cake. Sometimes they are trowel-shaped, and sometimes they have one raised edge, with the other flattened for cutting.

Left to right:
Strasbourg, 7¼″ (Gorham); Strasbourg [variation], 8½″ (Gorham); Florentine, 8½″ (Alvin); Rose, 8″ (Wallace); Specialty item, 9¼″ (no makers mark); Imperial Queen, 8⅛″ (Whiting); Dauphin, 8⅛″ (Durgin); La Marquise, 9½″ (Reed and Barton); Lancaster, 7¼″ (Gorham).

Ladles

Sizes of *Ladles* vary from tiny ones for mustard to the largest for punch. In ascending order, by size, they are as follows: Mustard, Mayonnaise, Cream or Sauce, Gravy, Bouillon, Oyster, Soup, and Punch. The smaller sizes adapt to serving almost any sauce or dressing, from oil and vinegar and Roquefort, to whipped or sour cream, fruit sauces, all gravies, au jus, hot-buttered or fruit syrups for waffles, pancakes, and/or French toast.

Bouillon or *Oyster Ladles* can also be used with small punch bowls or small soup tureens. *Soup* and *Punch Ladles* are interchangeable: the Punch Ladle has a longer, narrower handle and usually a smaller, lipped bowl than the Soup Ladle.

Brandy Ladles are as impractical as they are rare: they were probably used for flaming desserts. *Claret Spoons* (not illustrated) were probably used in tall crystal claret pitchers.

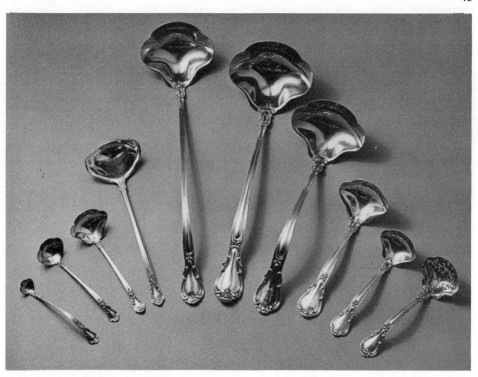

No. 1, left to right:
All the Ladles shown are in Gorham's Chantilly pattern, which was introduced in 1895 and has enjoyed unparalleled success: Mustard, 4¾″; Mayonnaise, 5¼″; Cream or Sauce [narrow handle], 5½″; Bouillon, 9″; Punch, 14¼″; Soup, 13″; Oyster, 11″; Gravy, 7″; Cream or Sauce [wide handle], 5¾″; Sugar Shaker, 5⅞″.

No. 2, left to right:
Mustard Ladles. Rose, 4¾″ (Stieff); Cottage, 5″ (Gorham); Strasbourg, 5¾″ (Gorham); Strasbourg [variation], 5¾″ (Gorham); Athene 5″ (Frank Whiting); Chantilly, 4¾″ (Gorham); Unidentified pattern [coin silver], 5″ (unidentified maker); Lancaster, 4¾″ (Gorham).

No. 3, left to right:
Mayonnaise and Cream Ladles. *Top Row* (all Cream Ladles): Plymouth, 5⅞″ (Gorham); Chantilly [narrow], 5½″, and Chantilly [wide], 5¾″ (Gorham); Frontenac, 5½″ (Simpson, Hall and Miller/International); Princess, 5⅜″ (Stieff); Strasbourg, 5½″ (Gorham).
Bottom row (all Mayonnaise Ladles): Strasbourg, 5⅛″ (Gorham); Unidentified pattern, 5⅝″ (unidentified maker); Chantilly, 5¼″ (Gorham).

No. 4, left to right:
Gravy Ladles: *Top row:* Repousse [handmade], 7½" (Kirk); Flemish, 7½" (Tiffany); Sir Christopher, 7" (Wallace).
Bottom row: Canterbury, 7" (Towle); Chantilly, 7" (Gorham); Strasbourg, 7⅜" (Gorham); Unidentified pattern, 7" (unidentified maker).

No. 5, left to right:
Pierced Ladles. Chantilly [small], 5⅝"; Chantilly [large], 6" (Gorham); Eglantine, 7"
(Gorham); Warwick, 7¼" (International); Kings pattern [coin silver], 7½" (Bailey &
Co.)

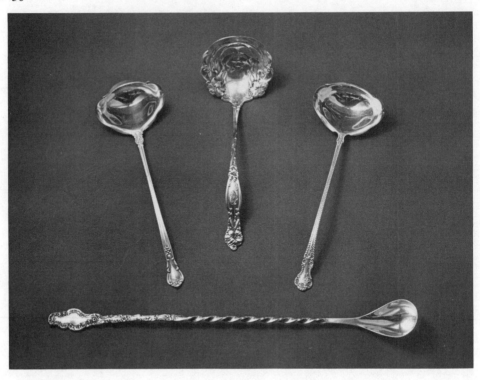

No. 6, left to right:
Bouillon Ladles. *Top:* Chantilly, 9″ (Gorham); Frontenac, 8½″ (Simpson, Hall and Miller/International); Cambridge, 9″ (Gorham). Brandy Ladle: *Bottom:* Watteau, 14″ (Durgin).

No. 7, left to right:
Oyster Ladles. Chantilly, 11″ (Gorham); Warwick, 10″ (International); Lancaster, 10½″ (Gorham); Alice, 10″ (Fessenden); Strasbourg, 11″ (Gorham).

Lemon Servers, Lemon Forks, Orange (Citrus) Peelers

In some very old sets, *Lemon Forks* were included with each place setting to spear a lemon slice or wedge and hold it with the fork while squeezing it over one's fish or into one's tea. Now used as a serving tool, they can also be used for pickles, olives, hors d'oeuvres, meatballs, and butter pats or curls.

Sliced-Lemon Servers can be used for serving meat patties, stuffed vegetables, dolma and sarma, and pastries.

Orange or Citrus Peelers are used for peeling all citrus fruits, and they serve that purpose exceedingly well.

Left to right:
Chantilly, 4½″ (Gorham); Repousse, 4⅝″ (Kirk) [Lemon Forks]; Essex 7″ (J.B. and S.M. Knowles Co.); Hope, 7¾″ (Howard) [Lemon Servers]; Magnolia, 5⅞″ (Watson Co.); Bead, 5⅞″ (Durgin) [Citrus Peelers]; Etruscan, 4½″ (Gorham) [Lemon Fork].

Letter Openers

Letter Openers were often an accessory item made to match many sterling patterns, and some companies still include them on their current lists.

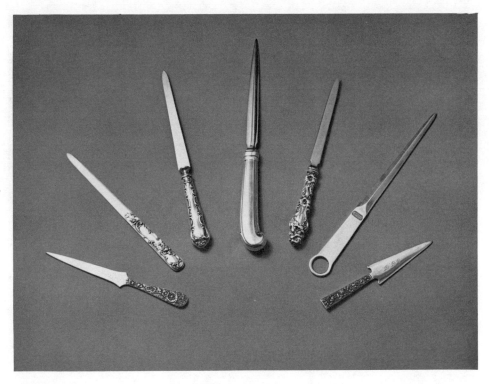

Left to right:
Repousse, 6″ (Kirk); Montclair, 6¾″ (Gorham); Strasbourg, 8″ (Burke/Gorham); 1810, 9½″ (International); Lily, 7⅝″ (Whiting); Antique, 8⅝″ (Reed and Barton); Repousse [handmade—listed as a "Paper Cutter"], 5⅛″ (Kirk).

No. 1, left to right:
Rosalind: Spoon, 9″; Fork, 9″ (International). Chantilly: Spoon, 9½″; Fork, 9½″ (Gorham). Norfolk: Spoon, 9¼″; Fork, 9¼″ (Gorham). Strasbourg: Spoon, 9½″; Fork, 9½″ (Gorham).

Lettuce Forks and Lettuce Spoons

Not every collector can locate a *Lettuce Fork* or a *Lettuce Spoon.* Even rarer are pairs. Either singly or paired, they are great for serving tossed leafy salads, spinach salads, coleslaw, Oriental dishes, individually molded salads, cauliflower, cooked spinach, deviled eggs, clams and oysters (steamed, stuffed, or

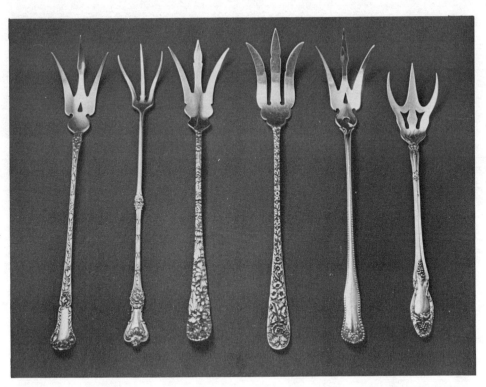

No. 2, left to right:
Lettuce Forks: Poppy, 9½" (Gorham); King Edward, 9¼" (Whiting); Princess, 9½" (Stieff); Repousse, 9½" (Kirk); Lancaster, 9⅜" (Gorham); Cloeta, 8¼" (International).

raw), fritters, fish patties, croquettes, dumplings, small whole potatoes, stuffed mushrooms, pattypan squash, and baby artichokes. Spoons alone can be used as pitcher spoons for lemonade or juices, as well as for serving pickled peaches, soft puddings, zabaglione, or whipped cream.

Macaroni, Spaghetti, or Fried Oyster Servers

As practical as they are difficult to locate are these large-toothed, or notched, servers. They are unsurpassable for serving pasta dishes, many entrées, cutlets or scallopini, stuffed pork chops, fish, and many vegetable dishes.

Left to right:
Chrysanthemum, 10″ (Durgin); Chantilly, 9½″ (Gorham).

60

Olive and Pickle Forks

Usually *Olive Forks* have two tines and *Pickle Forks,* three; however, this varies with different companies and patterns. In a few old brochures, some were even listed as "Butter Picks" or "Butter Forks" and they do serve that purpose well. Those with longer handles were intended for use with pickle casters or tall jars. Each can be interchanged with the other for similar purposes. Other than pickles and olives, they serve pickled herring, smoked fish, cocktail oysters or clams, onions, shrimp, crab apples, and any pickled or marinated fruits and vegetables. They also can double as lobster picks, and the short-handled ones as cocktail forks.

Fondue enthusiasts could collect them to use as individual fondue forks for either cheese (long-handled) or dessert (long- or short-handled) fondues.

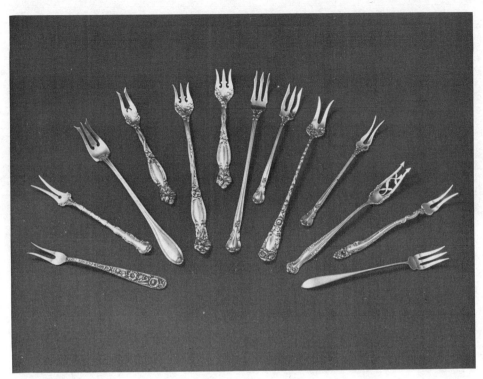

Left to right:
Repousse, 6" (Kirk); Strasbourg, 5⅞" (Gorham); New Margaret, 8" (International); Frontenac [Olive], 5⅞"; Frontenac [long-handled Pickle Fork], 8" and Frontenac [short-handled Pickle Fork], 5¾" (Simpson, Hall and Miller/International); Chantilly [long-handled Pickle Fork], 8½" (Gorham); Chantilly [short-handled Pickle Fork], 5¾" (Gorham); Chrysanthemum [long-handled Olive Fork], 8" (Durgin); Chantilly [short-handled Olive Fork], 5¾" (Gorham); Canterbury, 6¾" (Towle); Decor, 5⅞" (Gorham); Lafayette, 7¼" (Towle).

No. 1, left to right:
[All pieces are all-silver unless otherwise indicated] Strasbourg [plated blade], 10″ (Gorham); Beaded, 10¾″ (Bigelow Bros. and Kennard); Frontenac [plated blade], 10⅜″ (Simpson, Hall and Miller/International); Repousse, 9⅝″ (Kirk); Chrysanthemum, 9⅝″ (Durgin); Lancaster, 9⅝″ (Gorham); Lily of the Valley [stainless steel blade], 10″ (Gorham); Chantilly, 9¼″ (Gorham); Fairfax [plated blade], 10″ (Durgin).

Pastry and Pie Servers

Older *Pastry* and *Pie Servers* are usually all-silver, often beautifully pierced, patterned, or engraved. Some are quite wide and others, quite narrow, while some have a lipped or raised edge on one side or across the back. Some versions have plated blades and others, particularly the newer patterns, have stainless

No. 2, left to right:
Top row: Meadow, 10″ (Gorham); Chrysanthemum, 9⅝″ (Durgin); Unidentified pattern, 10½″ (unidentified maker); Chantilly, 9¼″ (Gorham); Lancaster, 9⅝″ (Gorham).
Bottom row: Repousse, 9⅝″ (Kirk); Bead, 9½″ (Frank Smith); Warwick, 10″ (International); Wellington, 9½″ (Alvin).

steel blades. All are extremely serviceable pieces for cutting and serving pieces of pie, cake or pastry, cheesecake, bombes and molded ice cream, or other desserts. Many can double for serving entrées: casseroles, stuffed or sautéed vegetables, and meats.

Preserve Spoons

An intermediate-sized spoon somewhere between a large sugar spoon and a small berry spoon, *Preserve Spoons* are occasionally referred to as either. Usually ornate or oddly shaped bowls distinguish these from tablespoons, but they can be used for any purpose for which a tablespoon is used. No longer available in current patterns, ardent searching usually turns one up in older patterns. Besides use as a tablespoon, they serve excellently on large buffet tables where many choices make smaller portions desirable.

Left to right:
Chrysanthemum, 7½" (Durgin); Raphael, 7½" (Alvin); Iris, 7¾" (Durgin); Chantilly [large], 8" (Gorham); Mother's, 7½" (Gorham); Chantilly [medium], 7¼" (Gorham).

No. 1, left to right: Olive Spoons
Top row: Chantilly [short], 6″ (Gorham); Jefferson [hand-hammered], 7¼″ (Lunt); Chantilly [long], 8½″ (Gorham); Canterbury, 8⅝″ (Towle); Norfolk, 8¼″ (Gorham); Repousse, 6″ (Kirk).
Bottom row: Rose, 6⅝″ (Wallace); Victoria [formerly Florence], 8½″ (Frank Whiting); [specialty item], 8½″ (Gorham); Lancaster, 8⅝″ (Gorham); Chambord, 7⅜″ (Reed and Barton).

Relish, Horseradish, and Olive Spoons; Chowchow and/or Piccalilli Sets

Horseradish Spoons usually have elongated, narrow bowls, although a few are rounded and others are somewhat shovel-shaped. *Olive Spoons* are oval and usually pierced, although not always *(see illustration No. 2).* *Relish Spoons* are variations of both the Horseradish Spoon and the Olive Spoon. These pieces are used interchangeably with chutneys, jams, honey, tartar sauce, hot or sweet mustard, marinated button mushrooms, and cocktail onions.

Oddly shaped pieces, but specifically designed for their purpose, are *Chow-*

No. 2, left to right:
Kings: [two-piece Piccalilli or Chowchow set] Fork, 7″; Spoon, 6½″ (Tiffany). Evangeline,* 6⅛″ (Alvin). Paul Revere, 6¼″ (Towle). Violet [short], 7¼″; Violet [long], 8¼″ (Wallace). Imperial Chrysanthemum, 6⅛″ (Gorham). Unidentified pattern,* 6⅜″ (R. Blackinton); Waverly,* 6¼″ (Wallace). Wild Rose,* 5⅞″ (Watson). St. Dunstan, [Chowchow or Piccalilli Fork] 7″ (Tiffany). La Tosca, 5⅞″ (Sterling Silver Mfg. Co.). 18th Century: Cocktail Fork, 5⅝″, Infant-feeding spoon, 5¾″ (Reed and Barton).

*It is uncertain whether these pieces are Horseradish Spoons or Honey Spoons.

chow or *Piccalilli Spoons* and *Forks.* Uses include relish, pickles, chopped onions, cocktail onions, mushrooms, sauces, jams, jellies, mustard, mayonnaise, sour cream, Parmesan cheese, and candied and stuffed fruits.

One can improvise by using an Infant Feeding Spoon or Jam or Olive Spoon together with a Cocktail or Pickle Fork, which are available in most current patterns. These pieces would probably be unpierced, but they work equally well. They are especially fun to use on the "do-it-yourself" hamburger or hot dog smorgasbord, where it is sometimes necessary to use several at one time.

Salad Sets

The elegance of a Caesar salad calls for a magnificent silver *Salad Set.* Useful for all salads, either piece can be used individually for serving numerous vegetables, meat, or casserole dishes. The Spoons can be used for berries, fruit cups, and compotes. The Forks also work well for meats, entrées, and some pastries.

Left to right:
Repousse: Fork, 9¾"; Spoon, 9¾" (Kirk). Strasbourg:* Fork, 9"; Spoon, 9" (Gorham).
Chantilly [new style]**: Fork, 8⅝"; Spoon, 8⅝" (Gorham). Melrose: Spoon, 8⅝"; Fork,
8⅝" (Gorham). Chrysanthemum: Spoon, 9"; Fork, 9" (Durgin).
Bottom: Rose [large Salad Fork], 9½" (Stieff).

*This same style was available in old Chantilly.
**Older style was also available in Chantilly and other Gorham patterns.

Salt Spoons

Salt Spoons and dishes (or dips) were made in two basic sizes: master and individual. The Master Salt Set was used at the table to fill individual salt dishes, which were then placed at each place setting. They are fun to use: one can be passed, or placed between place settings to be shared. They can also be used for individual portions of hot mustard, tartar sauce, soy sauce, or dipping sauce for fried shrimp. Pepper can be served in an individual dip as well, or in a pepper mill or shaker in conjunction with the salt dish. Larger sizes work well for individual portions of jam or jelly, especially on a tray for pampering a patient.

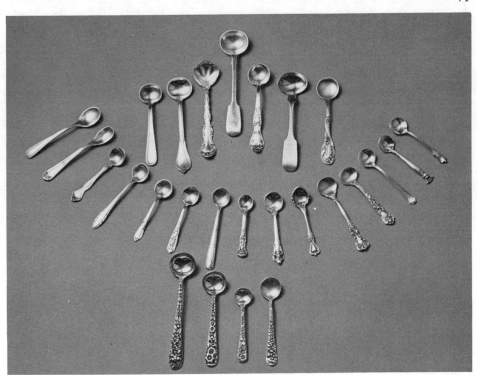

Left to right:
Top row: Master Salts: Calvert, 2¾″ (Kirk); Norfolk, 2⅛″ (Gorham); Strasbourg, 3⅝″ (Gorham); Unidentified pattern [coin silver], 4″ (unidentified maker); Unidentified pattern [coin silver], 3⅜″ (unidentified maker); Unidentified pattern, 3¹¹⁄₁₆″ (Simons Bros. and Co.).

Middle row: Individual Salts: Unidentified pattern [coin silver], 3″ (unidentified maker); Farnham, 3″ (Gorham); George and Martha, 2½″ (Westmoreland); Lyric, 2¾″ (Gorham); Rhapsody, 2½″ (International); Milburn Rose, 2½″ (Westmoreland); Camelia, 2¾″ (Gorham); Kings, 2¼″ (Tiffany); Grande Baroque, 2½″ (Wallace); Old Colonial, 2½″ (Towle); Revere, 2⅞″ (Wilcox and Evertsen/International); American Beauty, 2½″ (Manchester); Fairfax, 2½″ (Durgin); Romance of the Sea, 2⅜″ (Wallace); Grand Colonial, 2½″ (Wallace).

Bottom row: Repousse [Master Salt]; 3¾″ Repousse [old individual], 3″ (Kirk); Repousse [current individual], 2⅜″ (Kirk); Rose, 2⅞″ (Stieff).

Sardine and Anchovy Forks

Wide, short tines are indicative of *Sardine* and *Anchovy Forks,* the latter having the shorter tines. Sardine Forks may be used with marinated and stuffed mushrooms, sarma and dolma, pickled vegetables and sausages, and even petits fours.

Left to right:
[Sardine Forks, unless otherwise noted]
Top row: Kings, 5½″ (Tiffany); Unidentified pattern [Anchovy Fork], 4⅝″ (unidentified maker); Old Margaret, 5½″ (International); Pierced, [Anchovy Fork], 5″ (Weidlich); Lenox, 5⅜″ (Gorham).
Bottom row: Shirley, 5⅜″ (International); Paul Revere, 5″ (Towle); Chantilly, 5¼″ (Gorham); Floral [long-handled Sardine Fork], 7½″ (Frank Whiting); Chantilly [Sardine Fork(?)], 5⅜″ (Gorham); Strasbourg, 5½″ (Gorham); Chambord [Sardine Fork(?)], 6″ (Reed and Barton).

74

Spinach Forks

Spinach Forks, large and wide-tined, are most useful when spinach is cooked with leaves and stems intact. Few of these forks have been located. Probably only a few companies made them, and in a limited number of patterns. Foods other than spinach for which they are useful include steamed or stuffed cabbage, sauerkraut, baked potatoes, and meats, as well as for serving toast or rolls.

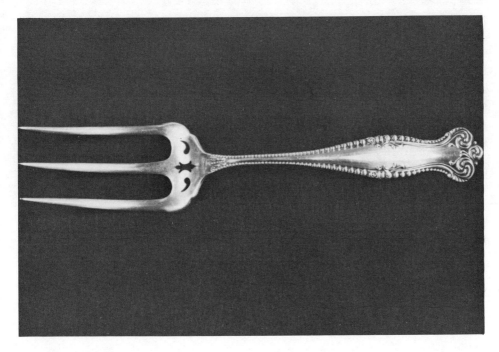

Canterbury, 9¼″ (Towle).

Stuffing Spoons

One of the most impressive items on the holiday table is a splendid, large *Stuffing Spoon*. Some companies formerly called these pieces "Platter Spoons"; others referred to them as "Casserole" or "Chafing Dish Spoons." They can double as serving spoons on a buffet table when a large bowl or a long reach is needed. They are essential for removing stuffing from the holiday bird, and elegant for serving same.

Left to right:
Fiddlethread [English, circa. 1843], 12¾″ (John and Henry Lias); Repousse, 12¼″ (Kirk); Medici [old], 12¾″ (Gorham); Baltimore Rose, 13″ (Schofield).

Sugar Spoons (Sugar Shells)

Sugar Spoons (sometimes referred to as *Sugar Shells*) are among the most versatile serving pieces made. Originally made in various sizes, some are quite large to go with the larger sugar bowls of the past. These are occasionally called small Preserve Spoons. Alternate uses suggested are for cream sauces, nuts and/or candy, jam, chutneys, cranberry sauce or jelly, relishes, condiments for curry dinners, mayonnaise, cottage cheese, dessert sauces, powdered cream, Parmesan cheese, whole pickled fruits and vegetables such as crabapples, kumquats, and beets, and croutons for soups and salads.

Left to right:
Top row: Eloquence, 6⅜″ (Lunt); 18th Century, 6″ (Reed and Barton); Dauphin, 6¼″ (Durgin); Strasbourg, 6″ (Gorham); King George, 6″ (Gorham).
Bottom row: Chantilly [plain bowl], 6¼″ (Gorham); Chantilly [fancy bowl], 6¼″ (Gorham); Daisy, 5½″ (Paye and Baker); Federal Cotillion, 6¼″ (Frank Smith); Decor, 6¼″ (Gorham); Rose, 6⅛″ (Stieff).

Tablespoons (Vegetable/Buffet Spoons)

The bowls of *Tablespoons (Vegetable or Buffet Spoons)* are individualized depending upon pattern and company. Some are fluted, ribbed, or flared; others are perfectly plain. They are indispensable on any kitchen, dining, or buffet table for serving salads, mashed potatoes, vegetables, and casseroles.

Sometimes still available in current patterns is the Buffet Spoon, which is easily interchanged with a Tablespoon. Paired with some meat forks, they make excellent salad duos. Pierced serving spoons also team with a regular Tablespoon as an efficient salad set.

Left to right:
Top row: Strasbourg [Pierced Tablespoon], 8½″ (Gorham); Early American, 9¼″ (Lunt); Lancaster, 8⅝″ (Gorham).
Bottom row: Chantilly [Buffet Spoon], 8⅞″ (Gorham); Eloquence [Buffet Spoon], 9¼″ (Lunt); Repousse, 9¾″ (Kirk); Kings, 8¾″ (Tiffany).

82

Tongs and Sugar Nips

Various sizes and shapes, from tiny *Bonbon* to extra large Sandwich and Asparagus, typify the assortment of *Tongs* available. Bonbon Tongs can be used for saccharin or sugar cubes. Larger sizes can be used for cocktail sausages, smoked oysters or clams, meatballs, cheese balls, cherry tomatoes, brandied chicken wings, sarma, or olives on the cocktail table, or perhaps as individual holders for quail or doves.

Very old, scissor-shaped Tongs were called *Sugar Nips* and were used for—literally—nipping off a piece of lump sugar.

Larger, bowl-shaped Tongs, known as *Pickled Peach* or *Ice Tongs,* work well with ice cubes, meatballs, stuffed vegetables, some sticky pastries, and any whole preserved fruit. *Sardine Tongs,* with flat and/or fork-shaped tines, lend themselves to serving tea sandwiches, herring, meat-filled pastries, turnovers, folded crêpes, and—of course—the large variety of sardines. Sandwich or Asparagus Tongs can be used for larger servings of many of the above.

Bar uses for various-sized Tongs could include ice, olives, lemon slices, maraschino cherries, and cocktail onions.

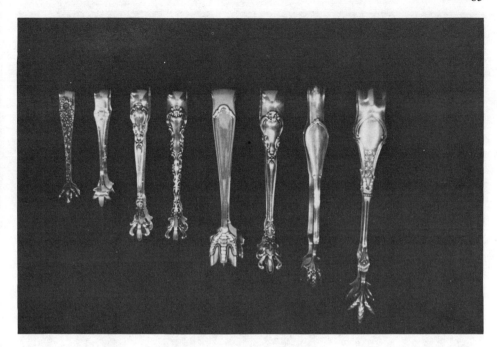

No. 1, left to right:
Repousse, [bon-bon] 3⅛″, (Kirk); Carmel, [bon-bon] 3¼″, (Wallace); Chantilly, [sugar, small] 4⅛″ (Gorham); Strasbourg, [sugar, small] 4⅛″, (Gorham); John Alden, [?] 4¾″, (Watson); Chantilly, [sugar, large] 5″, (Gorham); Cottage, [Ice] 5½″, (Gorham); Coin Silver, [?] 6½″ (not marked).

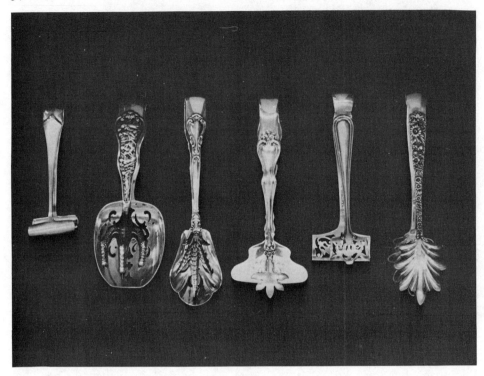

No. 2, left to right:
Unidentified pattern, [individual asparagus tongs] 4″, (European); Olympian, [possibly oyster] 5¾″, (Tiffany & Co.); Chantilly, [possibly pickle peach or ice tongs] 6⅜″, (Gorham); Hampton, [sardine] 6¼″, (Wallace); Commonwealth [sardine] 6⅝″, (Watson, Newell & Co.); Repousse, [ice] 6¼″, (Kirk).

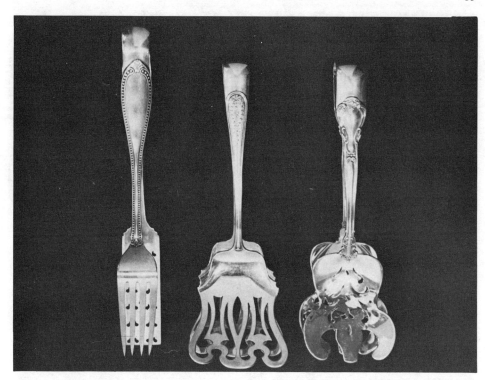

No. 3, left to right:
Bead, [sandwich] 10⅛″, (Whiting Co.); Jefferson, [sandwich or asparagus] 9⅛″ (Gorham), Chantilly, [asparagus] 9″, (Gorham).

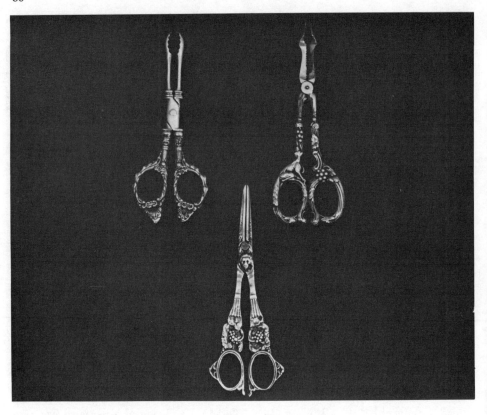

No. 4, left to right:
The top two items are Sugar Nips. The left item is 6″ in length and all silver. The second item is 6½″ long, with plated nippers made by Watson. The bottom item is a grape shear in all silver, 6⅜″ in length, with no marking.

What's Its

Left to right:
The small item in Dominick and Haff's No. 10 Pattern we believe is a *Pâté* or *Caviar Spreader.* The second item may be an *Orange Knife* in Apollo by J. B. and S. M. Knowles Co. The long-handled fork in Durgin's Louis XV may be a Lobster Pick. The last item is in Burgundy and was also made in Francis I, both by Reed and Barton, and it is a lemon fork.

PART II

Place-Setting Pieces

Introduction to Part II

Individual *Place-Setting Pieces* were as numerous and complicated as serving pieces. At one time, companies apparently vied with each other to see which one could come up with more pieces. All Place Pieces are adaptable to, or can be substituted for, today's less complicated settings. The attitude "How can I use it?" rather than "What is it?" is the more practical—and interesting— approach.

Individual Fish Knives and Fish Forks which, incidentally, work beautifully for fish, can readily be used for salad luncheons, casserole meals, and breakfast, or for any meal where a sharp cutting edge is unnecessary.

Many old sets have both luncheon and dinner knives and forks, which can be alternated on the table to serve large groups—serving the ladies with the luncheon size, and the gentlemen with the dinner size.

Cream Soup Spoons were made in both large and smaller sizes; Bouillon Spoons were the third round-bowl size. They work well for soups and stews and they can double for serving many dishes, especially condiments for curries, Mexican foods, and relishes.

Dessert Spoons also were made in two sizes; the smaller, now called the Place Spoon, was originally designed for puddings, cereals, cobblers, etc. They, also, can be used for soups and stews.

Iced Teaspoons are ideal for desserts in most parfait glasses, as well as for sodas and for stirring tall iced drinks.

Cocktail Forks were made in many different shapes and sizes by different companies, from Oyster Forks and Oyster Cocktail Forks, to Lobster and Fruit Cocktail Forks. (The latter are usually longer-tined than Seafood Cocktail Forks.) The smaller forks, such as Cocktail and the delicate, long-tined Strawberry Forks (see page 114), are interchangeable for oysters, steamed clams, and fruit cocktail, as well as the Lemon Fork, adapt well as cocktail picks or as serving pieces for canapés or hors d'oeuvres. The longer-handled ones work well for fondues. The larger, three-tined Oyster Forks can be substituted for dessert or pastry forks. Lobster Forks are usually claw-shaped.

Dessert Forks are more readily available than Salad Forks in some patterns and are perfect as substitutes for them. Pie Forks, Fish Forks, Fruit Forks, and both small and large Salad Forks can all be interchanged. For buffet service, Salad Forks teamed with some Butter Spreaders or Fish Knives can easily double the number of guests you can serve.

Rare and unusual are Ramekin Forks. The small, usually flat, short-tined forks were made for creamed or sauced foods served in individual ramekins. Today the same foods are often served in shells, and the Ramekin Fork is an ideal utensil. It is ideal, too, for many desserts, especially those frozen or jelled.

Ice Cream Spoons or Forks, more readily available than Ramekin Forks, can be used for any of the same purposes. Ice Cream Forks are especially well suited for eating pie or cake à la mode.

Nothing works as well as a Citrus Spoon for eating fresh California melons, as well as citrus fruits. These can also double for parfaits, sherbets, and puddings.

A grand finale for a fabulous dinner is a rich chocolate mousse, topped with whipped cream and served in individual demitasse cups with a Demitasse, Egg, or Chocolate Spoon. These spoons can also serve condiments and relishes, and they work beautifully for feeding the baby.

Place-Setting Pieces

The following diagrams from a pamphlet published by the Gorham Company, called, "How to Coordinate Sterling, China, and Crystal," show suggested place settings for breakfast, luncheon, dinner, and formal dinner.

Breakfast place setting, from left to right, using silver appropriate for the foods being served: Fork, Knife, Spoon(s), and Spreader on butter plate at upper left.

Breakfast

Breakfast forks are preferable, but luncheon or salad forks work equally well. If no fork foods are being served, eliminate the fork. The same procedure is applicable to the knife. If only breads or breakfast pastries are served, the spreader alone is sufficient. Spoons could include the following: teaspoon, dessert or place spoon for cereal; grapefruit (or citrus) spoon for melons or citrus fruits, some fruit compotes, papaya, guava, and other tropical fruits. If no grapefruit spoon is available, use a teaspoon. Supplemental pieces might include egg spoons, fruit cocktail spoons or forks, five o'clock teaspoons and ramekin forks.

Luncheon

Luncheon setting, from left to right, set for a semi-formal meal: Forks, Knife, Teaspoon, Soup Spoon and Spreader on butter plate at upper left.

Because luncheons, today, are so much more informal and lighter than in the past, table settings may not be as elaborate as this diagram indicates. Luncheon-size forks and knives are, of course, preferable and should be used if available, but place-size pieces are quite acceptable. Shown are Luncheon Fork, Salad Fork, Luncheon Knife, Teaspoon, Bouillon Spoon and Butter Spreader. Should the fare be simply soup, salad and bread or rolls, a setting with Salad Fork, either Cream Soup Spoon, Bouillon Spoon or Dessert Spoon, and Spreader would be sufficient. Optional pieces, according to the menu selection, might be Ramekin Fork, Fruit or Seafood Cocktail Fork or Spoon, Ice Cream Fork or Spoon and Iced Teaspoon, keeping in mind that the Cocktail Fork would be placed to the right of the plate in the order of usage. The Iced Teaspoon is attractive if placed perpendicular to the other silver under the beverage glass, or parallel to it to the right of the glass. If a seafood cocktail awaits the guest at the table, the Seafood Cocktail Fork may impale a parslied lemon wedge on the service plate. The Ice Cream Fork, or whatever piece of silver may be appropriate to the dessert, may be brought in with the dessert after the main luncheon dishes and remaining silver have been removed. There should be no place pieces remaining on the table when the dessert is served except the dessert silver and the Iced Teaspoon, or Teaspoon if coffee or hot tea is being provided.

Dinner, from left to right (the salad precedes the main course): Forks, Knife, Soup Spoon, Cocktail Fork, and Spreader on butter plate at upper left.

Dinner

Dinners today are as variable as the place where you live, the foods that you enjoy, the kind of cooking that you love to do, and the number and type of guests that you serve. More emphasis has been placed on entertaining dinner guests today than ever before, and countless magazines, food purveyors, organizational cookbooks, cooking classes, recipe exchange groups, cookbook book clubs, and gourmet societies literally bombard the interested public with new ideas as to foods to serve, suitable table settings and party decor with little "fuss or muss or bother." The keynote is "relaxed entertaining" with the host and hostess enjoying their party along with their guests. This contemporary type of entertaining provides as wide a leeway in table settings as it does in atmosphere.

Regional traditions are no longer absolute arbiters of correct usage, either in table settings and/or in specific culinary delights, although certain areas of the country may still excel in and emphasize their regional specialties. In the Western United States, for example, the salad is ordinarily served before the main course in a usual three-course meal, while in the East, it precedes the dessert. If the salad is served together with the meal, the salad fork should be placed between the dinner fork and the dinner plate. Starters, or appetizers, have been a fixture on the Eastern dining scene for some time, but in the West they are relatively new features except in the few classic established dinner houses specializing in French cuisine. "Southern Fried Chicken" has moved to Seattle and Texas-style "Barbecue," to Minneapolis; San Francisco's "Cioppino" to New Orleans, and Florida's "Key Lime Pie," to every kitchen in the country. As food preparation, serving and appreciation are being accepted as a significant part of our culture—coupled with the fact that more and more people are dining out today than ever before—dinner houses and private homes are becoming more internationalized and sectional traditions are fading before an onslaught of a vastly mobile and more informed public. Therefore, it can be said with some degree of certainty that there is no absolutely correct way to set a dinner table today. What are you serving? How are you serving it? Have a guest list of twenty and place settings for twelve? If you can't borrow, IMPROVISE! A buffet table can be set with ten Luncheon Forks and ten Salad Forks, ten Luncheon Knives and ten Butter Spreaders or ten Steak Knives arranged in effective groups. Men usually prefer the larger implements and women, the smaller. A Chinese dinner needs only a Luncheon Fork and Soup Spoon of your choice, and a spaghetti feed, a Luncheon, Dinner or Place Fork, Salad Fork and Dessert or Soup Spoon, and Spreader.

One of Betty Smith's most magnificent and successful dinner menus features her superb Cioppino, accompanied only by fresh San Francisco French bread and butter and a refreshing California table wine, with a light dessert and coffee. The table setting is simple: Cream Soup Spoon, Cocktail Fork and Butter Spreader. The Cioppino is served with a Soup Ladle from a large tureen into wide soup bowls and guests help themselves to chunks of French bread onto butter plates set with Spreaders. Dessert is, perhaps, a Frozen Daiquiri Ice served with Parfait Spoons. The preparation is minimal and can be done beforehand, and the table setting simple, elegant and comfortable, the atmosphere relaxed, and every guest and the host and hostess feels the evening a marvelous success, which it is.

Formal Dinner

Dick Osterberg's specialty is served in a more formal room calling for a more formal setting, starting with his famous Cream of Cauliflower Soup and continuing with his excellent stuffed, rolled veal, wild rice and asparagus with tangy hollandaise sauce. As in the European tradition, salad follows the dinner course and consists of fresh Greens garnished with delicate Herb Dressing. The table setting includes, Dinner Fork, Salad Fork, Dinner Knife, and Cream Soup Spoon. Dessert could be Fig Ice Cream served in delicate crystal bowls using ice cream spoons. Most of this meal can be prepared ahead with a minimum of last minute preparation allowing the host and hostess to mingle with guests, for a memorable evening.

Correct usage today, as pertains to dinner table settings, is primarily a rule of thumb: set your table according to what you are serving, how you are serving it, and how formal or informal you wish your dinner party to be. Your selection of place pieces can be as large and elaborate as your budget and your menu and your taste will allow, or as simple and informal as your life style directs.

A Formal Dinner place setting as shown by the diagram: Forks, to the left of the plate with Knives to the right of the plate. Note that there are no spoons nor a spreader. A Cocktail Fork is an optional piece, and if used, should be placed to the right of the knife on the far right, as would be the optional Soup Spoon or Teaspoon. These pieces should be placed in accordance with their usage during the course of the meal.

A special occasion still calls, occasionally, for a formal dinner, and allows one to use one's very best china, silver, crystal, and linen together with all the elegant accoutrements particular to a memorable occurrence. Since a formal dinner demands more courses, and there are traditional inviolable ground rules governing the presentation of such an event, the table setting should follow accordingly.

In the diagram, the place setting shows a Luncheon Fork, Dinner Fork, Salad Fork, Dinner Knife and Luncheon Knife. Luncheon size pieces are used for a first course, and could be used in conjunction with, or as a substitute for, a Fish Fork and Fish Knife, or Game Fork and Game Knife, depending on the number and/or kind of courses served. Soup Spoons and Teaspoons are optional pieces, as is the Cocktail Fork, again depending on the courses offered. The folded napkin is placed on the service place, and the buttered roll, directly on the table above the Salad Fork. Dessert Silver is brought in with the dessert. Silver should be set at each setting precisely 1-1/2" from the edge of the table and 1" apart from each other (use a ruler for best results). Glasses are set in a prescribed pattern: water goblet above the Dinner Knife, Red Wine to the right, and above, the White Wine and are removed together with the accompanying china and silver service at the completion of each course.

In England, all the silver used is present and in addition, the Salad Plate and the Bread-and-Butter Plate with a Butter Spreader is used. In France and Italy, as in most other Continental countries, it is the custom to place the silver face down, thus explaining the beautiful designs on the reverse of European silver.

A Formal Dinner can be an elegant theater for the host and hostess who wish to present their finest table furnishings, superb cuisine, impeccable service and unique ambiance to their most cherished friends.

Strasbourg (Gorham)

The Gorham Company, a division of Textron, furnished the following description of Strasbourg:

> A gay informal pattern from the luxurious period of Louis XV, inspired by the Rococo design of light-hearted scrolls with an occasional shell for balance. Its decorative scrolls increase in size to the top of the handle, and extending into bowls and tines, collect light and impart an unusual luster. . . .

The pattern was introduced in 1897, designed by William J. Codman, one of the leading designers working for Gorham at the time. He later played an important role in the design and production of Art Nouveau patterns for that company.

The illustration shows a six-piece place setting in the currently produced place size. The china is Coalport's Indian Tree, introduced in 1801 and still available. The butter plate has been omitted, upon which the butter knife would rest. Glasses would be placed to the right, above the knife.

Strasbourg *(left to right):* Place Fork; Salad Fork; Place Knife; Teaspoon; Cream Soup. *(Above):* Butter Spreader (hollow handle), which should be resting on bread plate. Salad in this case is being served with the meal; therefore the salad fork is preceded by the place (or luncheon or dinner) fork.

In addition to the currently produced basic pieces illustrated, the following pieces were available at one time and can still be found by the determined collector.

Left to right:
Knives: Dinner [French blade] 9½"; Luncheon [French blade], 9"; Steak, 9½"; Fruit, 6⅝"; Butter Spreader [flat-handle, all-silver], 6".
Forks: Dinner, 7⅞"; Luncheon, 7"; Salad [large], 6⅞"; Salad [small], 5⅞"; Ice Cream [new style], 5⅝"; Seafood Cocktail, 5⅝"; Ice Cream [old style], 4¹⁵⁄₁₆"; Strawberry, 4⅝".
Spoons: Iced Teaspoon, 7⅝"; Dessert, 7⅛"; Grapefruit, 5⅝"; Bouillon, 5⅛"; Ice Cream, 5¼"; Chocolate, 4"; Demitasse, 4".
Not shown: Place Spoon, which is slightly smaller than the Dessert Spoon.

Chantilly (Gorham)

Gorham describes Chantilly, introduced in 1895 and still one of the most popular patterns currently available, as follows:

Named for a famous French chateau, and a superb adaptation of Louis XV style, Chantilly is a cultured pattern of suave, graceful curves—one of the most famous flatware patterns in America. Characterized by movement throughout, the design has no straight lines. The reflective areas are bordered by rich ornamentation that extends into the bowls and tines. . . .

Chantilly (Photo on opposite page)
Top row, left to right:
Dinner Knife (or Place Knife, large) [old-style plated blade], 9⅝"; Luncheon Knife (or Place Knife) [French blade], 8¾"; Fish Knife, flat [all-silver], 8¼"; Fish or Salad Knife [hollow handle, sterling blade], 7¾"; Breakfast or Junior Knife [spatulate blade], 8¼"; Fruit Knife, 6⅞"; Butter Spreader [hollow handle, stainless blade], 6¼"; Butter Spreader [flat, all-silver], 6⅞".
Middle row, left to right: Dinner Fork (or Place Fork, large), 7⅝"; Luncheon Fork (or Place Fork), 7"; Pie Fork (large), 7"; Fish or Salad Fork [new style], 6⅝"; Breakfast or Junior Fork, 6"; Dessert or Salad Fork [small], 6"; Pie Fork, (small) 6" or Pickle Fork; Salad Fork [small], 5⅞"; Cocktail Fork [flared tines], 5½"; Cocktail Fork [straight tines], 5½"; Ice Cream Fork, 5⅜"; Ramekin Fork, 4¾"; Strawberry Fork, 4¼"; Lemon Fork, 4⅜".
Bottom row, left to right: Iced Teaspoon, 7⅝"; Place Spoon, large (or Soup or Dessert Spoon, now available in smaller size), 7⅛"; Cream Soup Spoon (formerly available in larger size), 6⅜"; Teaspoon, 5⅞"; Grapefruit Spoon, 5¾"; Ice Cream Spoon, 5⅝"; Five O'Clock Teaspoon, 5⅜"; Bouillon Spoon, 5"; Chocolate Spoon, 4⅝"; Demitasse Spoon, 4⅛"; Salt Spoon, 2¾".

104

Repousse *(left to right):*
Salad Fork; Bouillon Spoon (partially hidden); Breakfast Knife; Teaspoon; Iced Beverage Spoon. *(Above):* Salt Spoon.

Repousse (Kirk)

One of America's oldest silver patterns, introduced by Samuel Kirk in 1828, is Repousse. The pattern is currently in production and is described by the manufacturer as

America's first flower and foliage design. . . . The detailed artistry in design makes Repousse an incomparable pattern that will harmonize with any home decorative treatment. . . .

The illustration shows a Soup and Salad Luncheon Setting, using Royal Doulton's Burnham pattern china.

The following pieces are representative of a few of the items produced in this pattern. Although not shown in the illustration, the Seafood Cocktail Fork is currently available; it has shorter, more flared tines, and is interchangeable with the Fruit Cocktail Fork.

Left to right:
Fruit Cocktail Fork, 5⁵⁄₁₆″; Salad Fork, 6³⁄₈″; Luncheon Fork, 7³⁄₈″; Luncheon Knife, 9″; Tea or Breakfast Knife, 7⁷⁄₁₆″; Dessert Knife, 7″ [Note: Both the Tea and Dessert Knives bear an 1846 year mark and are handmade and all-silver]; Butter Spreader [flat, all-silver], 5¼″; Iced Beverage Spoon, 7⁵⁄₈″; Place Spoon, 7³⁄₈″; Teaspoon, 6″; Sherbet Spoon, 5⁷⁄₁₆″; Five O'Clock Teaspoon, 5⁵⁄₈″; Bouillon Spoon, 5¼″; Demitasse Spoon, 4³⁄₈″; Salt Spoon, 2½″.

Burgundy and Francis I (Reed and Barton)

The illustration shows how patterns can be combined effectively. Pictured are Burgundy and Francis I, both patterns currently being made by Reed and Barton. Burgundy was introduced in 1949, and Francis I, in 1907. Identical in shape, many pieces made in Francis I never have been available in Burgundy, which makes them ideal for collecting and combining the old with the new, the ornate with the classic.

The basic six-piece place setting is shown in Burgundy; the Cocktail Fork, Dessert (or Salad) Fork and Teaspoon (dessert service), in Francis I. Note that the Dessert Service is displayed in the European manner. The china is a Dresden floral by Carl Schumann, San Louis Rey. Water and wine glasses, not shown, would be positioned above the knife.

Left to right:
Salad Fork, Dinner Fork [both Burgundy]; Cocktail Fork [Francis I]; Dinner Knife,
Cream Soup Spoon, Teaspoon [all Burgundy].
Above: Butter Spreader [flat handle; Burgundy]; Dessert/Salad Fork and Five O'Clock
Teaspoon [Francis I].

Frontenac (Simpson, Hall and Miller, now International)

This is a highly-prized Art Nouveau pattern with lilies entwined with their stems in intricate design, introduced in 1903. The ornateness and depth of the design, plus the large selection of serving pieces, make this pattern highly collectable.

Left to right:
Cocktail Fork, 5½″; Salad Fork, 6½″; Luncheon Fork, 7⅛″; Dinner Fork, 7⅝″; Dinner Knife, 9⅛″; Luncheon Knife, 8⅞″; Butter Spreader [flat handle], 5¾″; Dessert Spoon, 7¼″; Cream Soup Spoon, 7″; Teaspoon, 5⅞″; Five O'Clock Teaspoon, 5⅝″; Coffee Spoon, large, 5⅛″; Bouillon Spoon, 5″; Demitasse Spoon large, 4½″; Chocolate Spoon, 3½″.

Left to right:
Fish Fork, 7⅛"; Dinner Fork, 7⅛"; Salad Fork, 6¼"; Dinner Knife, 9¼"; Fish Knife, 8¼"; Soup Spoon, 7"; Teaspoon, 5⅞". *Above:* Butter Spreader, 5½"; Ice Cream Fork, 5½".

Iris (Durgin)

Durgin's Iris is another Art Nouveau pattern, introduced in 1900. The outstanding dimension of design makes it extremely desirable. The illustration shows a placement of silver for a dinner that would include the following courses: fish, soup, entrée, salad, and dessert. The butter spreader shown above the forks would not be used in a conventional formal setting. This illustration also shows the effectiveness of an ornate old silver pattern, and a simple, modern china by Franciscan combined in a semiformal place setting.

Left to right:
Strawberry Fork, 4¹³/₁₆"; Cocktail Fork, 5⅝"; Salad Fork, 5⅞"; Luncheon Fork, 6¹¹/₁₆";
Luncheon Knife, 8⅞"; Butter Spreader [flat handle, all-silver], 5⅛"; Cream Soup
Spoon, 6¾" [large]; Teaspoon, 5¹³/₁₆"; Citrus Spoon, 5⅝"; Five O'Clock Teaspoon,
5³/₁₆"; Bouillon Spoon, 4⅞"; Demitasse Spoon, 4⅛".

Old Orange Blossom (Alvin)

Old Orange Blossom was introduced in 1905 by Alvin. A 1916 brochure states:

The choice of the orange blossoms as the motive of a design for sterling silver
tableware, is amply justified by the intrinsic beauty of the flowers as well as by its
traditional association with the marriage ceremony.

This was another turn-of-the-century pattern which offered many elaborate
and ornate serving pieces.

Chrysanthemum (Durgin)

Introduced in 1893, Chrysanthemum's ornateness was carried into the bowls and/or shank of every piece, except the stainless-bladed knives, if not on the front, then on the back. This aspect of its design has made Chrysanthemum one of the most sought after of patterns. Many of the great variety of serving pieces are shown throughout this book.

A German crystal cocktail glass, sterling fluted bread-and-butter (or sandwich) plate, and Heuchenreuter's White Racine china complete this place setting, except for the missing bread and butter plate and goblets.

Left to right:
Salad Fork 6¼″; Luncheon Fork 7″; Cocktail Fork 5½″; Luncheon Knife 9½″; Place
Spoon 7″; Teaspoon 5¾″, *Above:* Butter Spreader 6″, [hollow handle].

Strawberry Forks (Various manufacturers)

Adorable and unique, these small, long-tined forks are sometimes two- but most often three-tined. They were individual pieces designed for piercing a berry, dipping it into an accompanying dish of sugar or whipped or sour cream, and popping it into one's mouth.

These delightful pieces are really fun to collect and use as you would any pickle, lemon, or even cocktail fork. They work especially well as cocktail picks and for dessert fondues—and even as they were originally intended.

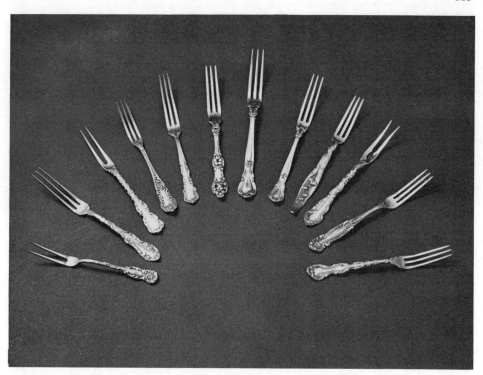

Left to right:
La Reine, 4¼″ (Reed and Barton); Old English, 5″ (Towle); Louis XV, 4½″ (Whiting);
Number Eight, 4³⁄₁₆″ (Simmons & Paye); Rosalind [old], 4¹¹⁄₁₆″ (International); Old
Orange Blossom, 4¹³⁄₁₆″ (Alvin); Chantilly [large], 5½″ (Gorham); Chantilly [small],
4¾″ (Gorham); Lily of the Valley, 4¾″ (Whiting); Rococo, 4⅝″ (Campbell Metcalf);
Emperor, 4¾″ (Mauser); Strasbourg, 4⅝″ (Gorham).

Left to right:
Top row: Pusher, Fork and Spoon: Strasbourg, 4½" (Gorham); Fork and Spoon: 18th Century, 4½" (Reed and Barton); Fork and Spoon: Forget Me Not, 4½" (Stieff); Spoon: Repousse, 3¾" (Kirk).
Bottom row: Pusher: King George, 3⁵⁄₁₆" (Gorham); Fork and Spoon: Chantilly, 4½" (Gorham); Pusher: Louis XV, 3½" (Whiting).

Baby Sets, Pushers, and Children's Silver (Various manufacturers)

Short, stubby handles enable babies to learn to use their own utensils. *Pushers* were made to help children push food onto their forks or into spoons without using fingers.

What nicer gift for a "newborn" than his or her own Baby Set?

Infant Feeding Spoons are individual place pieces used for baby's first solid

Left to right:
Strasbourg: Infant Feeding Spoon, 5¾″ (Gorham). 18th Century, 5¹¹/₁₆″ (Reed and
Barton). Repousse: Fork, 6⅜″; Knife, 7¼″; Spoon, 5⅝″ (Kirk). Lancaster: Fork, 6¼″;
Spoon, 5⅝″ (Gorham). Frontenac: Fork, 6″; Spoon, 5⅛″ (Simpson, Hall and Miller).
Columbine: Fork, 5¾″; Spoon, 5⅜″ (Paye and Baker). Chantilly: Fork, 6⅛″; Knife,
7¾″; Spoon, 5⅜″; Infant Feeding Spoon, 5⅞″ (Gorham). Royal Danish: Infant Feeding
Spoon, 5¾″ (International).

food. They lend themselves to many uses (see page 67 for additional uses).

Junior Sets are scaled smaller than luncheon-sized pieces and many substitute for adult Breakfast Sets. They are so sized in order that the child can learn
to handle "grown-up" silver properly.

Indexes

Index to Serving Pieces

Index to Place Pieces

Manufacturers Index

This index to manufacturers is not intended as a complete guide to identifying old pieces, but as a guide only for pieces used in this book. For a more complete list, refer to:

Turner, Noel D. *American Silver Flatware, 1837-1910*. San Diego: A. S. Barnes and Co., Inc., 1973.
Rainwater, Dorothy T. *Encyclopedia of American Silver Manufacturers*. New York: Crown Publishers, Inc., 1975.

Alvin Company
Gorham Division of Textron, Inc.
Providence, Rhode Island 02907

Amston Silver Co., Inc.
Division of Elmore Silver Co.
(Out of business.) Dies purchased by:
Crown Silver Inc.
48 Walker Street
New York, N.Y. 10013

Bigelow Bros. and Kennard
Now Shreve, Crump & Low,
Boston, Massachusetts 02116

R. Blackinton Company
79 Walton Street
Attleboro, Massachusetts 02703

Dominick & Haff
Acquired in 1928 by Reed and Barton,
Taunton, Massachusetts 02780

Durgin Company
Division of Gorham Company
Providence, Rhode Island 02907

Fessenden & Company
Providence, Rhode Island
(Out of business.)

Gorham Company
Division of Textron, Inc.
Providence, Rhode Island 02907

International Silver Company
Meriden, Connecticut 06450

Samuel Kirk & Son, Inc.
Kirk Avenue at 125th Street
Baltimore, Maryland 21218

Lunt
(Rogers, Lunt and Bowlen Co.)
Greenfield, Massachusetts 01301

Manchester Silver Co., Inc.
49 Pavilion Avenue
Providence, Rhode Island 02905

The Mauser Manufacturing Company
(Later part of Mt. Vernon
Silversmiths, Inc.)
(Purchased by Gorham.)

Mount Vernon Silversmiths, Inc.
(Purchased by Gorham.)

Paye & Baker
Attleboro, Massachusetts
(Out of business.)

Reed & Barton
Taunton, Massachusetts 02780

Schofield Company, Inc.
Baltimore, Maryland
(The Stieff Company manufactured some
Schofield patterns.)

Shreve & Company
San Francisco, California 94108

Simmons & Paye
North Attleboro, Massachusetts
(Out of business.)

Simpson, Hall & Miller
Wallingford, Connecticut
(*See* International Silver Company.)

Frank W. Smith, Inc.
Division of R. Blackinton Co.
79 Walton Street
Attleboro, Massachusetts 02703

Sterling Silver Manufacturing Company
Providence, Rhode Island
(Out of business.)

The Stieff Company
800 Wyman Park Drive
Baltimore, Maryland 21211

Tiffany
727 Fifth Avenue
New York, New York 10022

Towle Silversmiths
Newburyport, Massachusetts 01950

Wallace Silversmiths
Wallingford, Connecticut 06492

Watson Company
(*See* Wallace Silversmiths.)

Watson, Newell & Company
(*See* Watson Company.)

Weidlich Sterling Company
Bridgeport, Connecticut
(Out of business.)

Westmoreland
% Wallace Silversmiths
Wallingford, Conn. 06492

Whiting, Frank M.
% Crown Silver Inc.
48 Walker Street
New York, New York 10013

Whiting Division of Gorham
Providence, Rhode Island 02907

Wilcox and Evertson
(*See* International Silver Company)

Patterns Illustrated

128